Crooked at the Far End

Editor: Brenda Schmidt
Cover art: Richard Gorenko
Illustrations: Hayley Peters
Book and cover design: Tania Wolk, Third Wolf Studio
Printed and bound in Canada at Friesens, Altona, MB

The publisher gratefully acknowledges the support of
Creative Saskatchewan, the Canada Council for the Arts and SK Arts.

creative SASKATCHEWAN   Canada Council for the Arts   Conseil des Arts du Canada   sk arts

Library and Archives Canada Cataloguing in Publication

Title: Crooked at the far end / by Gerald Hill.
Names: Hill, Gerald, 1951- author.
Series: Hill, Gerald, 1951- Man from Saskatchewan ; bk. 6.
Description: Series statement: The man From Saskatchewan ; book 6 | Poems.
Identifiers: Canadiana (print) 20200301349 | Canadiana
(ebook) 20200301357 | ISBN 9781989274415
(softcover) | ISBN 9781989274422 (PDF)
Classification: LCC PS8565.I443 C76 2020 | DDC C811/.54—dc23

radiant press
Box 33128 Cathedral PO
Regina, SK S4T 7X2
info@radiantpress.ca
www.radiantpress.ca

The Man From Saskatchewan, Book Six

Crooked at the Far End

GERALD HILL

"real age...was variable, crooked, capricious,
singing here and sullen there..."

- Donna Tartt, *The Goldfinch*

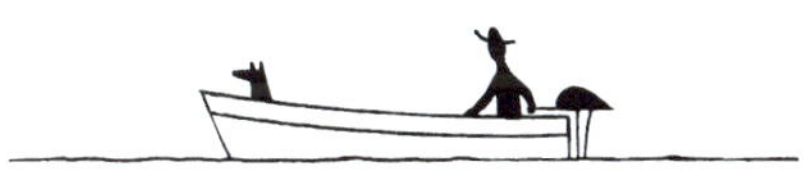

Contents

Invocation

Morning gets here wet. The night bleeds
mist and wind. I pack whatever fits
in my father's jacket—a jacknife,
tin of smoked meats, vital creams
and lotions. He'd say
after you've sat long enough,
get up and go.

His jacket, a GWG, hangs
from a kitchen chair, west-bound.
I'll finish my pot of tea, leave a note
for care of the house, lift my arms
into the jacket and go.

Morning is a bright-eyed
goddess in disguise, the river
a thin road to an iron bridge.

Let us know, Muse—what tumbles
from the hills this morning. What thought-rocks,
what bones? Look, prepare yourself,
earth is your witness. A man who was once a boy
is setting out.

Eight Souls Who Shared 1927 to 1930 on This Planet, and the Odd Happy Hour in a Cabin at Emma Lake

Hold your guests up as examples to your children.
– Gustave Flaubert

Marilyn Monroe, Movie Star

Knocker, knocker. The minute she enters,
the room reads polkadot white dress
tight at the knees, white blonde,
dark in one eye, scared in the other,
swallowing hard candies whole.

Give me the smokey, the free, she says,
crossing to the dresser stacked
with rum, beer, pineapple, rye.
We're scenery she moves with her eyes.
Lots of ice, please, she says.
She's about to sit down.

She chooses the divan, well I have no
divan, it's an extra bed and wool
blanket or two. *A tick swelled in my foot,*
the size of a blueberry. She waggles
a white pump. *This one. I'm stung,*
the beauty of this spot. Say, do I know
you fellas? Here she laughs. *Take it easy, boys,*
rocking her shoulders back. Our breath
does what hers does.

Listen, the wind off the lake
cracks in her glass.

E.G. Hill. Grandfather

Butts his cane at my door, smoking his pipe.
I let him in. *Thank you, sir,* says he.
I don't know what accent. He's thicker
than I imagined, whiter through the beard.
The sun is a warm one today. He takes a rum
in a hand stronger than mine. *I was forty-five*
by the time I got to Saskatchewan
by train, three children, winter. I froze
my whiskers off getting to the farm.
Five more children in the next twelve years
in a house I built,
good years except for the last ones.

He walked forty miles to get here, he said,
and that was nothing.
A man at home with a single chair,
he likes his own company.
Only wind can make him laugh.

He won't have another rum right now, thanks.

He tries my peanut-and-cheese hors d'oeuvres,
seems fussy, won't stay long. One stout
handshake, he's gone.

Virginia Woolf, Writer

Arrives by hackney cab
a half hour early. I've barely swept
the doorway, cut the rind off
days-old cheddar. She's seated
like folded leaves facing one way,
thinking another, *the thought of hours,*
she admits when I inquire.

Today's light begins dark
and surfaces, one line
pushing the other. She sees
through my polkadot curtains,
a torrent of leaves lit or shadowed.
I slip a cup of tea to her seizing mind.

The party turns, she's fixed
at the eyes to a tremor
I must cross, she says,
tightening her wrap. The wind blows
this room of her long skirts.

Later I spot her
down by the beach hucking stones.

Jack Kerouac, Writer

Digs what roads do, wheels
a '54 Chev right up to the cabin,
grabs his smokes, heads in.
Almost sundown when he shows up.
Over there, pointing to it.

Talk about quiet—he parks himself
by the window and darkens in his flannel
shirt (sleeves rolled up, been bitten
out there, I see) and jeans,
sneakers. Talk turns to loneliness.
We talk, he's lonely, downing wine
soaking from a fringe of clouds
sadder than ever, then *Yeah,*
he says, *Yeah!* By God he's writing
his "Sundown Sutra" on the back
of his pack of Luckies he tosses
my way as he leaves. It begins:
that fever through the eyes today was light.

Brother B., OSB, Monk

Appears just when I've put things away, lined up
my shoes, set out the radishes and baby dills.
First thing, he's a chuckler. Second, he hands me a pail
of berries, looks the place over. *Come on* he says.
I've got half an hour for Cribbage, your deal.

Saw a doe and two fawns,
wish I'd seen them sooner.
Right out there. He points
with one hand, slaps down
a double-run of three with the other,
fifteen-four and eight's a dozen.
They were mule deer
not white-tails, he says. I'm busy
counting my hand, pair of queens is all.

I'm skunked in minutes. He works
the cards as if dealing for a front-end
loader tractor. I'd pray but what good
is that when the cards won't hear.

Whatever you need to know,
B. can open with his jackknife
and lay down his cards
and bury you.

Ella Fitzgerald, Singer

Listens, a big fan of breeze or reeds
brighter by the word. She picks up
swing in no time, greets
warmly the room just now entered.
Sure, I'll try the rye, she says, *I'll try*
the rye and scatters
laugh in a song
when she sings it.

She goes by
moon but maybe the moon is wrong
the moon is wrong
the moon is a chorus
a calm
boat and should lightning strike—(snap)
god forbid but should lightning
strike—that'll be Ella
loose with her band.

Robert Kroetsch, Writer

Worries about too much sun, he says,
in his white hair, white beard,
old as hockey legend Gordie Howe
and golf legend Arnie Palmer,
sitting in my cabin with a beer.

Kroetsch is to blame for today's light
which splinters and flares for his arrival
in his horsefly tractor, his bucking dock.
Twelve hours earlier, a football moon
scored behind a blade of sprucetop.
I'm writing poems, he says. *I love it.*

Half-way through his beer he recalls
with a laugh a man he'd seen
swimming in a slough, wind
blowing in the swimmer's mouth.
Must have been a farm kid,
thinks he's found the Riviera.

This lightly clouded day after solstice,
twenty degrees in wind and blue,
we're indoors far from the trembling.
No mosquitoes in here, he says.
It's good to just
sit for a while.

Marlon Brando, Actor

Holds a banana to his ear, a cellphone
he bought at Fern's Grocery and Event Centre
at Murray Point. *Cost twenty bucks. Here, try it*
and we pass around Brando's
banana-phone, eyeing his blond ponytail
and Japanese print cocktail robe
from the folds of which he pulls
a Sony MP3 recorder the size of two fingers,
and headphones he cuffs on me.

I hear Brando walking the path from Fern's
speaking of mosquitoes and water
dropping from the high leaves,
musing on puddles and clouds
reflecting each other. Once he calls
Jimmy Caan by banana-phone
but can't get through, bugs too busy.
He pulls at the lock of an empty cabin,
has to admit the softness of air
is beautiful—all this recorded
in footsteps, a few words.

Later he has us look through
skylights, tipping our heads back.
We eat berries, drink, peer at the world
through the roof of a box
someone set at the edge.

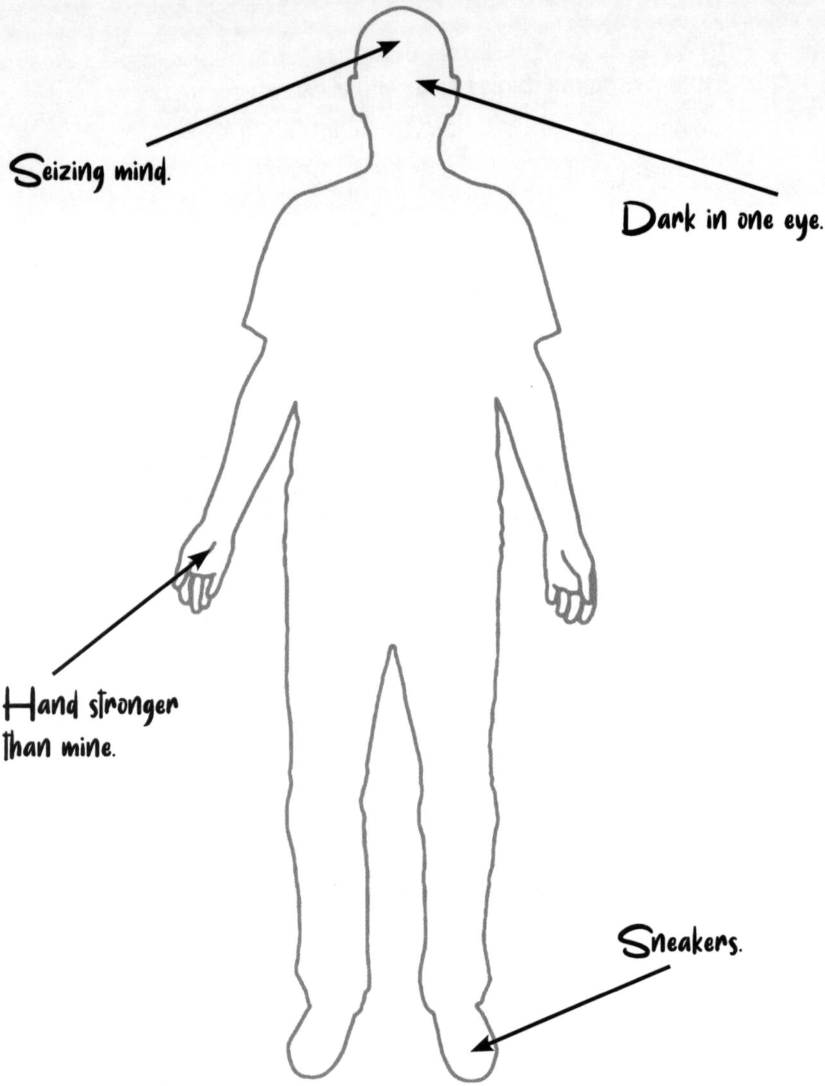

Scenery She Moves with Her Eyes

Natural Cause: A Mountain Notebook

Page of Water

Mud-rich, dragonfly daddy
lousy with breeze, I could breathe
a lake full and empty. I could catch
and eat the quiet things,
give my body air.

I could spark my birdsong motor,
preen and eat till the stars come home,
could dissolve to sand, come back
as current pressing the bottom
of a feel-good canoe, come back *heard.*
I and the bunchberries pacing
each other's sightpath could fake petals,
stir or carry cloud debris,
run for blue, tell shadows what
tomorrow's sky will see. If rain
picks up I will draw myself
in rainstrokes if I want to or sleep.
O how lovely the sleep sensation,
nothing but natural cause.

Page of Train

I fill a page with emptiness
known as love, known as naked
body on the 6th floor lounge. I go on
like that, magpies torturing mule deer
and squirrels and years ago
my cat Purina (who purred when
I ran a bath) so dumb she'd follow me
to school. Hey, I've found--
what's the word--a *sequence,*
portrait of the artist as a young
old man—the bullying, the play, the sharp fears,
first named, then as the series
might develop, deeply revealed.

That much takes about a page. I'm tempted
beyond the walls of this ravine.
Ravine it, that's the key. Downhill
take the hoodoo trail to the river. Look
tourists crowd the viewpoint, shhhhhhhhh
one's about to speak. I reach my hand
into water so clear, I don't
hear the train. Shhhhhhhhhh, the train.

Page of Blue

Shape comes from where you put it, not where
you got it. Mind + world = mind,
a foreground of spruce,
a hundred more up a ridge
and back, and through them
Sulphur Mountain.

I imagine my body half-fallen, tied with ribbon
marked *Pest Control.* The spruce lend
their missing-bark bodies to green
brown, yellow and what I mean
when I say *bright blue.*

Page of Deadfall

What I know of *Martes americana*
I can see right now. The rest I look up,
claiming the marten's project as my own.

Climb or take your prey along the ground.
Lope, wear a dark-brown body
much-prized. Prefer
old-growth coniferous. Stay curious
for voles, hare, shrew, grouse, and other
forest lunch.

I feel the marten's steep decline
in abundance. Hawks and owls
prey on marten but I myself
am its worst enemy, I read, ruing those peels
I pitched up the slope the other day.

Look, the marten has followed deadfall
out of sight. So long, brother, say I,
loping back inside.

Page of Mountainside

Uncle Elk the mule deer feeds
in the ravine, seldom lifting
from his business. I hear a stream of urine,
a few tearing sounds from Uncle's mouth
and occasional flaps of Uncle's long ears
(the left tagged in orange plastic) against his collar.

In a fuss along a path come painters
from Berlin in their slappy shoes.
A whole night of elk couldn't imagine the racket
painters make, liquor bobbing
in their bags. Uncle Elk pulls grass,
teeth big as butterflies, tongue sweeping
juice away. In parentheses
there on the mountainside I count
the number of steps a painter takes
in twenty seconds past my studio,
times eight or nine painters
five or six times daily
three or four summers in my life so far.

Uncle Elk has eaten out of sight. *The mother*
leaves the baby here or under a deck
and picks her up later—I saw them nursing,
one of the painters says, getting it wrong
about Uncle Elk.

Page of Mauve

Writers are slow learners.
– Robert Kroetsch

As the novice acquires wisdom
the master reveals, so I learn
from poets on the Spray River
trail one afternoon. Is this
rutting season for the elk
or for the raven? Which is louder? *Should* we
get behind a tree? If I see a cougar, do I
(a) make a face and back up
(b) pretend I'm shadow
or (c) appear bigger—*yes that one!*
cry the poets. They reach for their stones,
their pocket tools, poet hats and pens,
and fine books. *Fight back,* they shout. *See?*
No cougars here.

And what about this plant, I ask—low clusters,
thick with needle-leaves. *Hm-mauve*
says a poet, putting her mind on what she sees.
Juniper. Medicinal, think gin—applause
from the poets—*but it's not a true berry.* Well,
true is a downer. The poets darken,
bow their heads, turn silent through their bodies,
their wild and ever-curious alpine hearts.

Page of Beginning

Seated on a rooftop minding the valley
I was body of light, a width and depth
forty miles up the valley,
mountains on four sides, river
train and highway slipping through.

Far above,
in a predator's ecstatic spree,
the cougar drags its kill.

I swing my notebook open and begin.
How endless the darkening, then a pause.

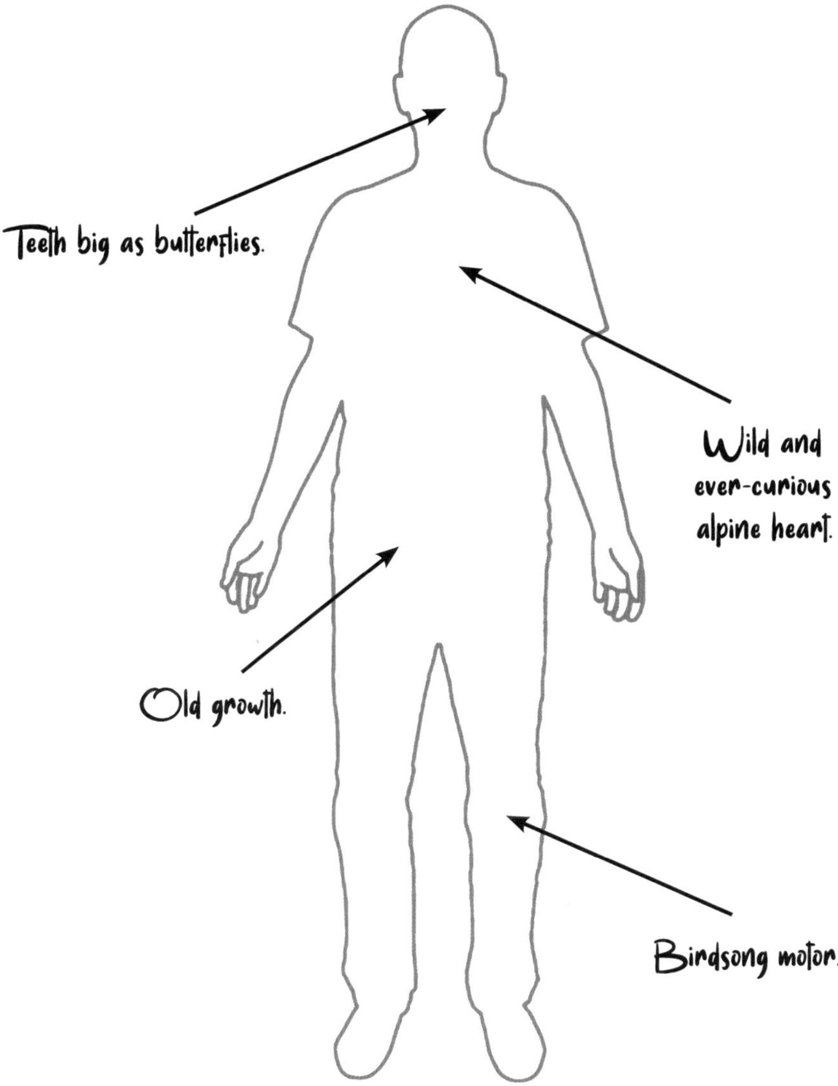

Dragonfly Daddy

Pub Scrawls

The Deep Inn

The Deep Inn is open all night
and only then. Its currency is dream-shapes
of silver, bronze, the front lawn of your friend
Rick's place on moving day, the dinner table
at which Charles Laughton (as seen
in *Witness for the Prosecution*) leaves
toothmarks on your pewter knife and you're some
Marlene Dietrich in a long black dress.

Most people here just died or found themselves
together in a room. Your old friend Clair seems hyped,
you can't keep up with her, she wants to play
with dials on the office telephone.
Another friend turns movies into books.
Your daughter's a small girl swimming—
fragments you empty onto the table
like coins for Crow Lager, the Raucous Ale.

Customers stand at the bar and shout
their roughest dreams at The Deep Inn,
slagging each other that way, throwing
glasses like live grenades at the big-screen TV
when the poor referee—whose dream
is he?—gets it wrong. The bigger the man,
the louder feckin' dream you feckin' hear
through to the lounge side,
an empty chair beside you where your own
night shines.

The Grand-Dad Inn

for Davey Alistair Warren

If you've heard news of a birth at home and felt
a tumble in your heart, if you've walked one way
in the last few minutes then the other or thrown
your cap into the air, take your seat
at The Grand-Dad Inn and lift your glass.
"To the wee bairn, Davey by name.
May he live true as the oak at Horse's Hill."

"Ay," the other grand-dads say, through mighty
heaves of lager. "May all he imagines
come to be" (here a further rip of lager). "May he grow
into men like us"—at that a pause,
each man living again his reel
of foolish choices, silly words.
"Ach, never mind. May wee Davey
grow to love these happy afternoons
with his mates," a point on which all agree,
heaving the next pint of Old Crow, one eye
on the door of the Grand-Dad Inn—
a lift of voices at the latch, the door opens,
and all the grannies come running in.

The Look Back Inn

Memory's free tomorrow
at The Look Back Inn. Today pay
your two pounds seventy-five to flip
through your notebook and write yourself
half-way through your pint, recalling
the woman in Guimarães singing fado.
English? she said. *I hope you like it.*
I already do, you said.

At The Look Back Inn you're just in time
(that's all you are) for the Pub Quiz:
When was last night? How sweet?
Is it time to go?

Please respect your neighbours
at The Look Back Inn.
This is a residential area.
Please remember responsibly.

The Stone Arms

You rub your eyes in your yawn chair
impressed by the gentlest breeze,
how skin when you touch it gives up
tiny grains of grey at The Stone Arms.
Chairs, tables, faces of old men—
everything stone, and the stone walls
drowsy. Even the beer takes
forever to pour.

By its own measure it's a busy place
of constant weather, the wearing away.
Here's the indentation where your grand-dad sat,
where he sang his one song, told his one
story a hundred times. *I'll see you
when you're better dressed,* he calls
to his mate Jock. *Ach, that'll be a long time.*

Unless it's hot you're cold at The Stone Arms.
By night you'll want the fire waiting
in the hearth for you. For a good time
think of what's-her-name whose lips
damn near burned you the night
The Stone Arms closed and she and you
opened the fire in each other's skin--
well you made that up except
the night.

The Sycamore Or Less

You dance at the Sycamore Or Less,
shake your beauty round to rough tunes
the Catkins play. You dance,
with Persons Under the Age of 18,
the blind guy on the Polton Mill bus,
whoever comes through that door
looking for the ancient boogie a tree
like you performs, your arms
crooked and your feet so thick.

You dance and burn the Scottish light
for hours at the Sycamore Or Less,
you free-form thing. The Catkins
lay down that Old English *bōc* rock,
that Old Norse *bók* rock,
the whole Germanic dancing *book*—
and here comes Jane, straight from washing
her MG. Soon she's washing the floor with you.
You've seen branches move like she does, all give
and bend and flutter. *I cannot help it,* she says.
I've always loved to dance but hurt myself
two years ago. Doing the splits, I fell
at the Sycamore Or Less.

The Easy Flynn

Breathe a scatter of starlings, tint of ash,
the silent work of being watched by deer
in Scottish wind and all the winds
that ever blew.

Open the gate, walk a narrow road,
stone walls bent with hedge, and a stable.
A horse in blankets calls another horse
out for a ride. *Go easy, Flynn,* the rider says,
patting the neck of her mare.

That narrow road, Skodas zooming by at 65.
Beneath your feet the wind has left
the rubbish of a late spring storm. Here comes
the number 41. The man in the front seat is blind.
You heard him last night in The Easy Flynn complain
of a horse blocking the road to Polton Mill.

Walk that narrow road, a choice
of wrong turns, of bus, of "public bar" door
or "lounge" door, choice of lager (5p more
on the lounge side) and whether to open your book
or not, the hard work of a word in this wind
burying tree-tops, shake and shiver, *Easy, Flynn.*

The Inn with the Rest of the Names

Call it The Windy Inn
        that pushes you
The Troubled Arms
        folded there
The Shirt and Trousers
        for looking good
or The Sunday Underwear.

Call it The Olde Log Inn
        for that joke you tell
The Mudslide
        ‘cause it’s good and dirty
The Spoon and Porridge
        at 8 o’clock
Blue Sky by eleven thirty.

Call it Beam
        if you fancy single words
Jim’s Beam
        if your name is Pat
Jim Beam’s Folly
        if your roof’s too high
Jim Beam’s A-Falling after that.

Call it Book of Dreams
        if you've opened one
A Line of Rock and Stone
        on page ten
The Head and Pillow
        all night long
The Wish I Had a Longer Bed

Call it That's Enough
        if it ever is
A Line Or Two More
        when it's not
The Place Where Some
        Canadian Had
An Afterthought.

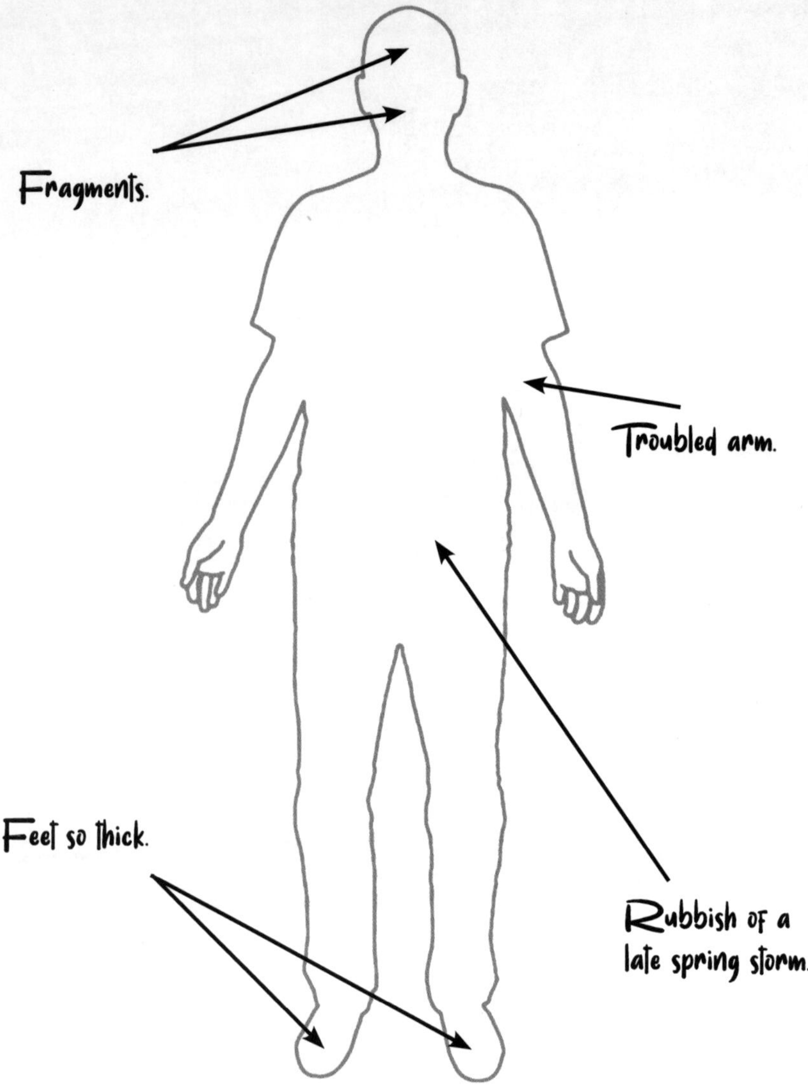

A Tree Like You

Occasional Cities

Better the long way home, than home.
- John Ashbery

It is the sun that shares our works.
- Wallace Stevens

I just saw two Romans smoking in the doorway of the Mercado.
- Stan Still

Scene at Graça Viewpoint

I'm hungry after the world,
troubled beyond my own haze warping
unevenly these last billion years.

What particles left me? Why didn't I notice
what time my body began
to cool over the evening terrace?

Will I ever see thirteen billion
years like these ones? *Finally!* I say
every trillionth of a second, my arc

just beginning, my telescope, my hundred
billion galaxies. No wonder I get lost through
narrow streets. If this stays true, whew I'm dark,

dark matter! This trauma
eases. Don't I speedwalk
to the viewpoint, see past

the bridge into the—
what is that, distance? Look, my beard
pre-dates the earthquake. Look,

I sit on a bench at the viewpoint
in a weary overcoat and flat cap,
scarf and shiny shoes.

Lisbon, Portugal

Anecdote of the Shower

This morning emerging wet,
beautiful as I'd ever be, I heard sirens.
What drama is this, I wondered, not yet dry,

parting the curtains of my fourth-floor room.
Death-cries of a peacock torn apart
by a fox in an olive tree?

Wild Renaults scraping the south and east
walls of Cathedral Sé?
Some ruined *fadista* singing

the wreckage of his love?
When I stepped onto the balcony,
naked as an empty chair facing

south to the sea, on the *Rua*
dos Bacalhoeiros men abandoned
the football scores, a woman hurried

children into her KIA, cafés
that had opened now shut
their doors, and could it be—

yes truly—the great ships had deserted
Lisbon harbour.
When I leaned over the railing,

the senhora across the street
looked away. Pigeons flew up without
the usual flying down. One by one

the orange trees withheld
their ancient fruit and trucks
their fresh bread

until I turned to the curtains and took
my body damp and simple
back inside.

Lisbon, Portugal

Evening Tram to Rossio

Trams slow,
tracks curve or taxis
block the rails.

I'm the one
curving. Get to the end,
I hop off. All day

it rains. Maybe it's the wine
I'm about to drink, two euros
a bottle.

This morning I caught
BBC World Service. Pakistan will never know
Kashmir again. The tram

moves slow or topples. I start a page
and down the hill to Rossio turn it,
filling the square with birds

hopping on tables.
I'm the quake of '14 though
nothing yet has fallen.

Lisbon, Portugal

Are We in Trouble?

Who invited the Wasp-class
amphibious assault ship USS Bataan
to the harbour where the great ships,

truly heroic ships set sail. Is rust
the new grey? Quick
nightfall save us from the blunt face

of 'ol 44, its mooring ropes sick
of their own oil scrap. Officers
of Bataan disembark, a-clatter,

saluting their BMWs.
Men and women of 22
in shirttails and shaved heads sign

at the top of the gang and head down,
a night ashore, Bataan a fragment
of bulky shield, rust aglow.

Give us not
heroes descending, nights
in shining, soon to be drunk on cloud.

Lisbon, Portugal

City of Right Size

I find along the avenue late
one afternoon an empty box
of the right size.

I note its provenance
as carton of butter and stuff it
into my bag with the baguette

and lost onion and head
straight home minus one
turn right and lock my door.

I have found the right size for a package
sealed against any parliament, regent,
republican guard, hotel

manager or postal agent,
in short accessible only to
myself at some future,

should there be one, when standing
in my doorway I observe
approaching in City of Right Size

a box . . .

Jerez de la Frontera, Spain

Anecdote of the Flamenco Show

He found himself seated
in front of a woman as unlike any other
as he was any man. She sat alone

in her jeans and pale blue jacket.
She remained still, arms folded,
perhaps chilled for the day

had been rainy, perhaps stealing herself
against further distress, for he had noted
shadows in her face. The show

ended. He made his way to the back
and down the steps. There she was
walking up the empty street

as was he, the only footsteps.
He drew even and offered his arm.
With unusual vigour she took it,

pulling herself against him. In this manner
they passed the cathedral,
turning left for half a block then right.

Still they said nothing. By the time
he could see the sign for his hotel
he'd grown uncertain. It was then she stopped

before what was apparently her house.
She unlocked the door and drew him inside.
That much he knows is true.

Jerez de la Frontera, Spain

Map of Sevilla

Plotted in sector G4, I peel and share
an orange by the curb. Fiat Calientes
pass and scooters and bikes

and, first its shadow, a brown and white
pony pulling a cab. Last night
I folded into districts torn down the middle

of E5. I'd gathered at street names
available, a dimension
at a time, most of them happy

though last night over in C4 my leg
acted up and I might have left a tapas bar
without paying. Blame flamenco

down the alley, way down
the alley. I see myself true
as paper in your left hand

next to your cup, a document
under your seat. See if I'm not so.

Sevilla, Spain

Rebecca of the Dark Morning

The sun will reach Rebecca on the north side
of the street at noon, the lingerie
shop where daughters wait and mothers

pat their hips at the shapewear
in the window. 25 Euros
for the gel bras, 5 or more

for knickers the model wears.
Rebecca herself appears in her doorway
pulling out her phone and her glasses

to see it. A father's left
hand grips the boy's right
at the same place the faithful bore

Christ on the cross past the shop
during Carnival. By 12 bells the sun
would be lapping at the stylish brown

leather of Rebecca's shoes had she not
vanished into the drama of her shop.
If I could, I'd nudge

sunlight to Rebecca.
How sunny she would be.
How dark on the south side.

Cádiz, Spain

Liberation

for the Carnation Revolution that dumped the Salazar regime,
Portugal, 1974, and for Lucy, who joined me in celebrating, 40 years later

Not a shot was fired
April 25th 1974,
climbing on tanks and gunboats

and kneeling beside rifles. They told us
to stay inside but we heard music
and ran to our flowers and cast them down

to encourage the generals
and free ourselves.
The tyrant after forty years must fall

on his own heart kept alive
in false news two more years.
How we sing now the rain

of carnations, every window
slick with it. So sweet
is our remembering that music.

Lisbon, Portugal

Living Better

The bull runs away as mighty head
mounted free of the wall of some bodega
and spends his last terrors

in a ring. Meet Inclusero, owned by Zaluendo
or Lionardo, killed by Morante de la Puebla.
April 21st 2006 this happens

in the ring at Sevilla. Horse and bull
dress up their brains until one of them dies.
After in our restaurants we chew

at casseroles, lean to our wines
in the shadow of toro 126
whose head the size of a chesterfield

rules the lusty planet Inclusero.
Here's to transience. We live better
savage than true.

Sevilla, Spain

Love Poem Contest. Second Prize

Where the sea sings its rapture at the shore,
we love. In the wooden elec-stasies of trams,
we love, the tiny wheels and curved track

and the one long arm that draws the charge.
Three women under one umbrella in wide
sunglasses though skies are dull, these women

in the dark coats and silk scarves we love.
The dogs for whom love is water
we protect with our love. Ascending any staircase

with a key to any room we love, in our single beds,
single rooms, secrets of our bodies
we love. Hands over our eyes in the middle

or should we say depth even death of night,
no sound from the street but traffic
of screams, we love.

Potatoes near our plazas we love,
knowing these treasures like love
will be consumed. Square-headed stones

underfoot we love, numerals and letters
of licence plates, children calling from
inside their walls, all bells, all cathedrals

spires and domes, all prayers we love.
We still and always love the tender fits
language endures, lost souls asleep before the gate.

Smokers in doorways lighting the streets
with brief flames we love. Every time
a poet forgets a word or turns

away refusing, we love.
In the sweetness of view, the gaze upon the city,
on every street we love again

all the way to the sea.

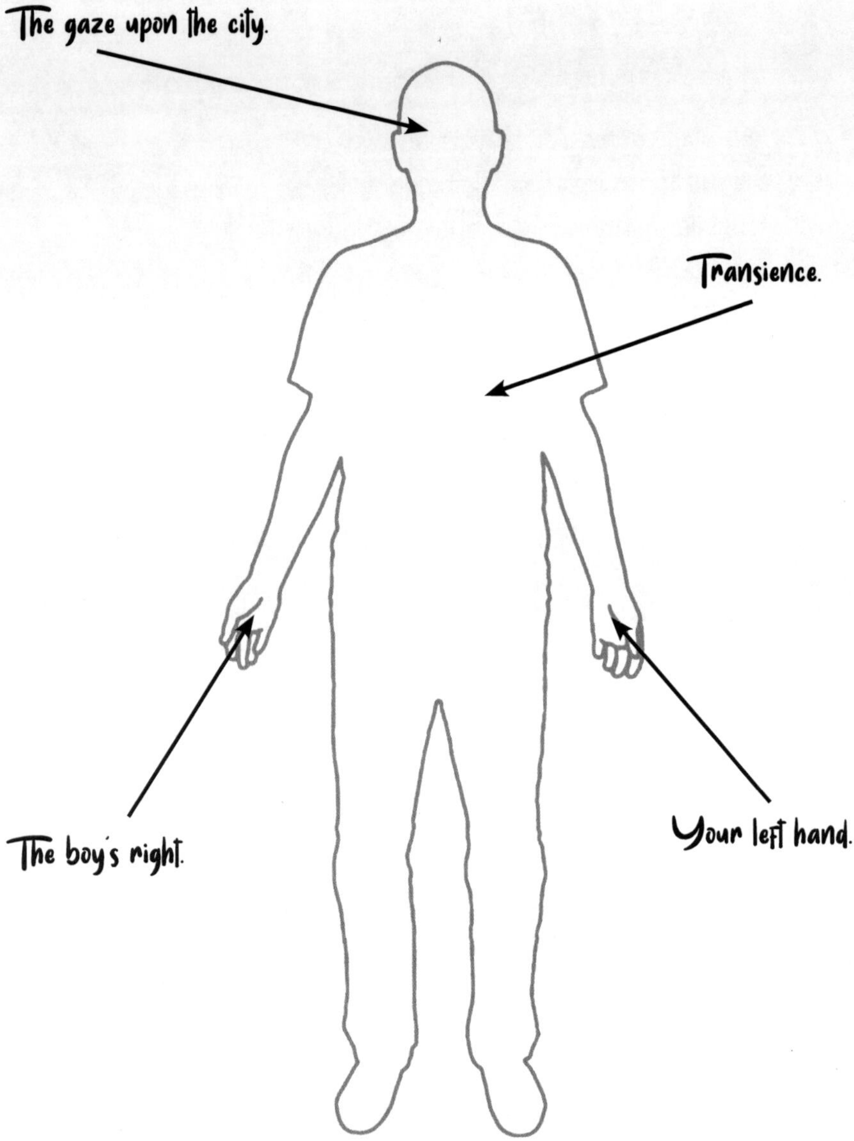

Dark, Dark Matter

Songs for Scarborough Bluffs

Billy Van's Cottage

You paid five thousand in the 70s
for a cottage on the Scarborough bluffs
knowing bluff-all except 90 metres up
gives good horizon. You painted the cottage
blue for the lake, blue for the sky
in the lake. What the hell, blue
was your mom's favourite colour.

Kitchen porch and living room,
bedroom off the back. You could wake
as if returning from weeks
on islands, waves before and after.
You could sip away.

Some days fine dust swirls
off the cliff face, taking a while
to *mean,* you reckon,
millions of years. Dreams
crash at the base of the bluffs
and a barn and log house vanished
last year. Things become unstable.
Nature courses. *Every time I come here*
more has fallen you say,
living toward the day it finally goes.

Moon

That recent moon took geese and squirrels
but left the holes, took hawk
and cloud left scatter
and flag and fountain, took night,
left horizon in the living room, left
a film of moondust on the table wiped
yesterday, took a word away
umbra from the kitchen, took mac
left the cheese, took arthritis
left the knees, took the sign left the dew.

That recent moon took the haircut
left the head, took your body
left your bed dragging
dreams around, took sun
left rise, the sea
and apples fallen. Took the coffee
left the tea, took page seven
left page three.

Gates Gully

From your shy cottage
where cabinets don't work and shelves
are empty and saws dull,
what honours you've won shut away,
now or then when the tv works,
you're on.

Pick the odd train, you're on it.
Throw a ball, you bring it back.
What are you doing chest high
in lake Hystereo? Just this afternoon
you saw a dog in a drycleaner's
window. It was Saul, Bernie's corgi
catching a snooze. Get off the subway
there you are with coffee
checking your compass for home.

You and landscape—one's a shine
on the other. You're blown away
already for all we know,
which we claim from our point
where the bluff meets
the gully is not much.

Fool's Paradise

for the painter Doris McCarthy

Free-meaning geese practice
feeding and repose. If you want
to run them off by clapping
your notebook or dissing them in Latin,
they feign scurry (brief dip
over the bluff) or indifference,
no cocking of neck, no fearsome
wingplay, no goosing.

The geese give you the tailfeather,
rip at grass further over. That pond
Doris built in '64 for the light and breath
we're given on this planet turns goose bidet,
preen-city for a dozen or more
Branta canadensis sipping or airing out
their wings in the pool of view.

Pump clogged with goose shit,
lawn mined with turds the size of mice—
too bad. You can stay inside, write down
your turns of praise for pond, lake, sky,
all of God's creatures but the goose.

If you could matter to a goose,
you wouldn't. Any goose
would tell you: you're the bad guy,
we're just eating apples.

Mirror

Addicted, you install a dozen mirrors
in your 800-square-foot house in which half
the walls are window. You're a red shirt
in every mirror, ducking through a doorway
like St. Francis himself composing
a prayer to a cat deceased or some dog
struck by lightning and left to live.

Blame it on your brain. Brain it! Why settle
for one horizon. Your grim mug
at rest heaves its love. You squint
a couple of cloudbones pressing
a fleshy sky.

All night darkness drains
nightpaths through the house.
Angels pass through an oval
frame as light.

Wind

Claiming to love wind, you compose
a piece with trees bending,
flag nuts on its pole, bluff dust
in your moustache, the ends of which want free
left to right from your face. Outside
is inside a singing wind you saw first
as whitecap blinks from southwest Toronto,
eyelids socked in lake Ontario.

You zip up your jacket seized large,
wind no longer warm through
the pocket. Everything moves
when you're sand and clay.
The last of a tree wraps
sharp-shinned hawks by the hundreds.

That roar in the mapletops is you ablow.
Here we are here we go
in this wind who will know.

Anecdote of the Otter

An otter with a mouthful of slime
gives you the eye one stiff afternoon
on a six million dollar breakwater below
a Scarborough bluff. You suppose
you could scramble to the top
if you had to. What a way to go,
buried upside-down in ten thousand years
or pinned by the root to some tree.

Waves this benign afternoon play at forever,
giving time and taking it. Earth falls
to pieces. One of these ages we'll all
dust away decomposed in clay
and sandstone to Toronto Island.

You're not sure whether to feel
such effects or notice them,
either way silent but for noise
of being seen by otters.

Borrowed Time

Lovers stroll for photo op
with wedding dress.

The lake pursues the fallen
up slabs of shale and through low trees.

You have scrambled there
and back yourself.

Love brings the bluffs down faster.
Look at the fragments.

Now the lovers take their clothes off
a metre or two from shore. They fuse,

refuse the past above them, the risk
they take, quick to crumble or dissolve.

Don't expect to see them
a million years from now.

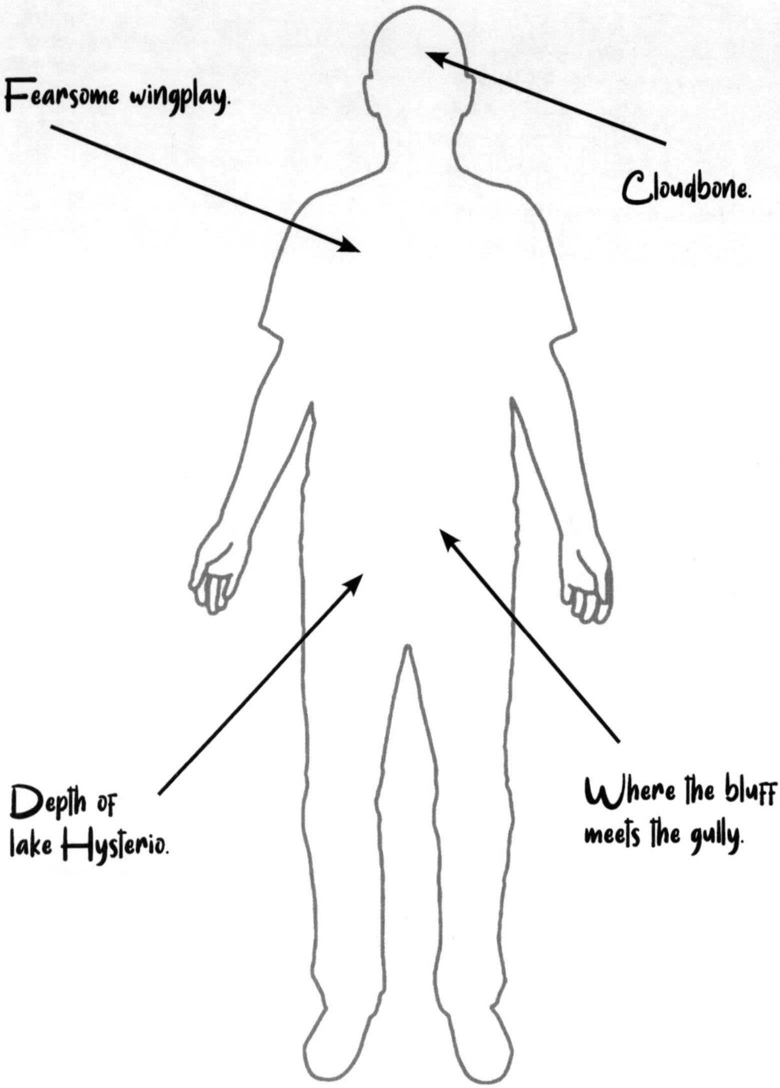

Some Dog Struck by Lightning

Writing Wrongs

Writing Wrongs

Wrong About the Morning

Nothing lagoons like tomorrow. When sunburn calls,
stubble it. Shine your back legs, word-like,
patient when the shadow's good.

Sam, you snorkeler—the woman next door
is the woman next door. On the way
to morning, the drums fall. Silent go
the sailors. Long and sandblown, a Christian
taxies tardy to the church. Some pajama
fools you, plastic in the sun-chained hour
between ten and rooster.

Slip the menu, *desayuno*. I'm not eaten.
From the tables a flat erupts, smell of sorrow
running from the right. My neighbour's dog—he's not
a neighbour but it's a dog—works the shit to the honey wagon,
a dog-and-rooster's *agua residuals.*

On Niños Héroes the cost of fooling goes up.
I turn the burner spine-ways but cool is out.
Uncle Tony reaches for his wife's fingers.
I've never seen him so timeless. Two seconds this takes.

Outside the curve songs,
take a whole sugar, why don't you.
Anything else? A drink?

Wrong About the Beach

I came to my angle by ship from Cozumel.
It was dotted. The reef turned camera.
Cancel my description. It should have been Sunday,
the reef simple. We took
a couple of boats out the short door.
You're the next island, wind-ship, deepener.
I can't bake but my skin's hot.
For a couple of pesos I'll be the law.

Who sits here and why
under overturned half-shells, bumping with blue?
Catalina, you sell me. Skip the ship,
take the house for a sunny wagon, not very
wise for a lighthouse. Those two times
you saw me, I bobbed.

Days like weather when the flags are good.
That homicide in Iceland, can we chase it,
hands free? We're sure to be tortugas.
Please, let pelicans need.

Wrongs About the Plaza

In the jeep called tractor, a rut bakes a wheel.
The shirt coming yellow, is it blue? You look like food.

If we were now a rowboat pacing, who would come to mean us?
Let me be your parked car.

I told a taco to its face the light was lime-green.
Whose idea was the boulevard?

Commercial properties will get it, sick.
Bike it or not, bodega.

Chairs come from sitting here.
We call it a sundress, I get it.

Says the next federale, there's machine gun.
In the silence of church bells the species totter.

For you, not us, the streetpalms flower.
Cut the ha-ha, this is spoken Saskatoon.

Lime alone cannot be eaten.
Fountain is the look I want for you.

The park is nowhere near the park.
The sea in morning reminds me of that town.

Wrong for the Great-tailed Grackle

All the years have dreamed us rotten.
Heal me in your empty sling,
            bird with yellow eye.

Fries in paper surprise the dead
Santa Fe woman, oh her.
Song me tender, school-tail,
            bird with yellow eye.

To define is callous, Marie didn't
happen dark brown. I stall
at your order, your slight riding-by.
Spear me,
            bird with yellow eye.

Work a dime less.
Swear by the water that takes us in
            bird with yellow eye.

Wrong About Myself

I trickled through, so precise
was the size of my shirt, the faithful
rinse my hair endured, brined for a million and a half.
Our cat died when I was seventeen.
I brought her outside from inside and watched dad
put her in the trunk. He was coughing. She belonged.

Saskatchewan, I'm footsteps, the airplane birded.
Said to be maybe, I'm a prince.
I pull my trance up early. And while the children swing,
I feel you, far and away, splendid to me.
Look behind the frost, my nice side.
Boost a *naranja*, manage my knees.
My skin is yours Saturday. Tell the sloop
of my neck about living, do. Trousers,
say I love you.

Wrong About Kisses

kiss the pelican glide
kiss the wife checking her husband in his kayak
kiss the kayak
kiss the thought of volleyball
kiss the oil on the bellies
kiss the smile
kiss the *policia* and Lisa and Sirena
kiss the lounge chair island in the hot-white sand
kiss the 2-for-1
kiss the great-tailed grackle
kiss the soldier's yawn
kiss the black trombone
kiss the burn
kiss the red flag
kiss the sag
kiss the money
kiss the hat off
kiss *oscura,* dark bohemia
kiss the breeze and the Mayans
kiss tomorrow
kiss the time it takes
kiss her ankles, let me
kiss like that
kiss me right on the stanzas
kiss the frigates when they come this slow
kiss the slow
kiss the carry of the bag
kiss the change

Wrong About One Night

Once when once was, we heard a wrecked moon and pitied
its bottom half. The chance of a journey
kept us home. I spoke up: You going to be fun
to notice with that rash of yours, tattered on the side?

I was thinner than I used to be, beanier.
The rules gave me run-around. The dream-truck
wept for the seen moon, bicycles, sand. Ok?
No wonder but plenty of sin, all told.

In the staircase, prophets trembled.
In the field, tools survived.

Wrong About Lorca

My eyes grew light, the first one dawn.
A trauma got me stashing my net.

Once in my anymore, in waves of Lorca I spoiled,
tried to dive but lifted, burning in every eye, azul too.
I wondered in umbrellas Federico reserved
for his solitudes. I gave myself an age. Speak *to* him,
I mooned: For this and all moments, Federico,
light is the surface your boats will remember,
sick and tending their grand alone.

Oh Susie Q, Federico—her bodies exposed like speedbumps.
I don't care what I look like walking away. Yikes, Federico.
Half-past twelve is eleven.
Surge, protect us!

Wrong About the Road

Fast George, that's got to be a motor. Heavens!
Where do you drink? It is spin that sits you?

Tenderize the half-life and this is what suspenders.
Oh my, what seconds. Quick! A woman ascends.

She'll someday shank us porous. A couple of evenings
won't hurt that single bird, shovels tell me.

Assassins come too. That semaphore is grandma-size,
deacon of sprang. Spreeking of ding, hell is poor cut Styrofoam.

It won't fly, this day of yours. A couple of Pepsis
rock Spadina. Flip a few, you'll seal it.

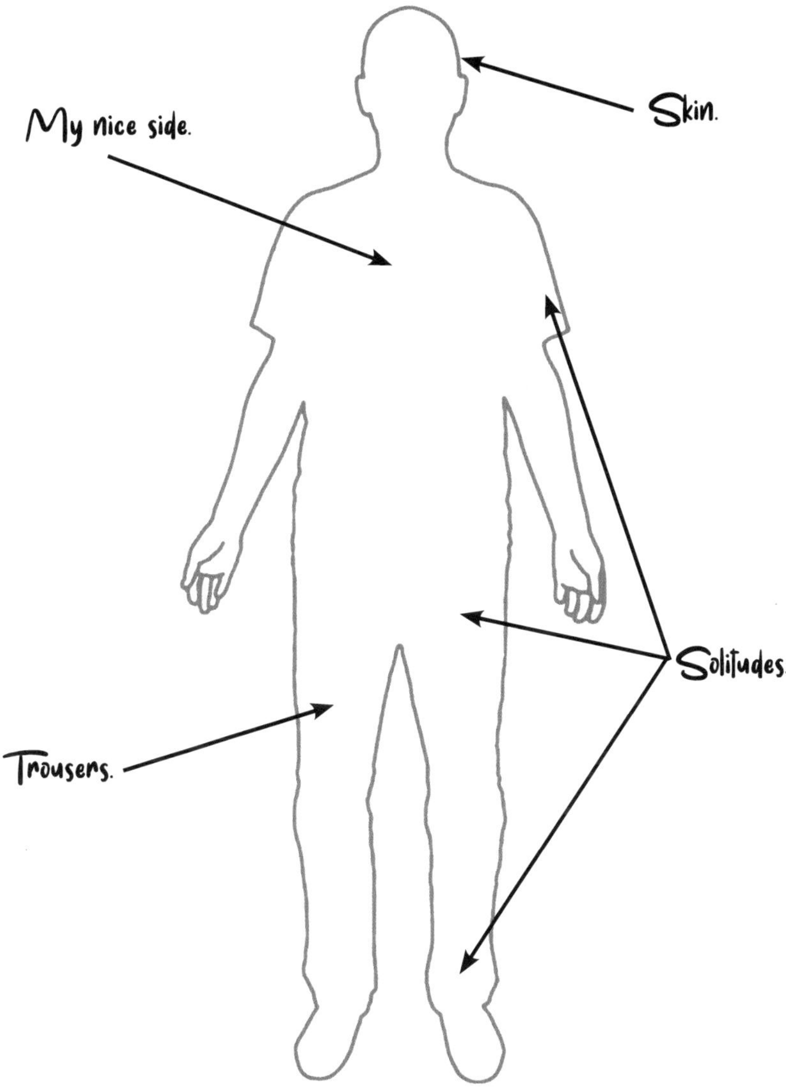

The Look I Want For You

When I Become Poet Laureate

1.

When I become Poet Laureate, we pause at the corner,
cocking an ear. We hear fado music from the hallways
of Government House, flamenco downtown,
jazz in every bell tower, and bluegrass
at rush hour. Fashion-wise, citizens wear
the hottest brand in retail: *Saskatchewear*,
stylish, easy on the black. On streets
or sidewalks clear of snow no one slips.
Early morning roars to life. All lights stay green
except the red ones. No matter what the traffic,
we get home.

When I become Poet Laureate, every goose sings like Adele
and confines its defecation to a rocky beach
east of the city. No turds the size
of cabbage rolls, no hissing.
Geese refuse all offers of bread.

When I become Poet Laureate, we all lose twenty pounds.
We look good. Sharp duds decades-old
spring onto hangers, ready to wear.
This very outfit reaches from my closet,
takes me in its arms and legs and out the door
and here I am. Thanks to the outfit,
the songbirds return, and the bees,
sweeter than ever. The Wellness
Index for Living Daily, or WILD, rises to its highest level
in a hundred years. Every man, woman,
child finds the slumber they deserve.

"Another hour of sleep? Go ahead" becomes policy
in the workplace province-wide, as does
Daylight Sleeping Time. In schoolrooms,
we all find our teachers, and they the assignments
lifting those who write or grade them to peaks
of knowledge and delight. Over vast tracts
of affordable housing, landlords speak
without memos, and listen
to their tenants: *What do you need?*
say the landlords. *Would you like*
a new stove? Do you mind
if we adjust your rent
down?

2.

When I become Poet Laureate, every friend
I've ever had (except the ones I'd crossed off)
comes for dinner prepared without fuss or panic in my
contemporary kitchen (as seen in
that hot new décor mag, *SasKitchen)*. I serve
bison with rhubarb sauce, wild rice
and Palm Springs cake. We eat
and drink and hug and accept all blame
for what has or has not come between us.
We say with perfect clarity
what we should have said years ago
and part, hope renewed, again as friends.

Our stores of verbal disasters
accrued over thousands of private
whispers or public rants are forgotten.
Where before we could pick any time
of day, occasion, classroom, bedroom,
living room, boardroom from here
to the furthest shores where we had spoken
words childish, cruel, stupid, ill-timed, so wrong
we'd never be right, now these traumas
have floated away. Bad memory
has left the province for good.

3.

When I become Poet Laureate, the provincial cabinet
arrives for daily briefings to my apartment
on Lorne. Over bran flakes and bananas
we reverse the slide in oil prices, then sit
around and read poems that offer love,
fear, joy, terror, the works, in many voices—
all of them good for the soul
and good for the Canadian dollar.

In every home, Saskatchewan books
open next to Dickens and Louis L'Amour.
And all citizens
have the right
to bear language.

4.

When I become Poet Laureate, our children
go to bed, fall asleep and emerge from dreams
fully dressed, fed, ready for school. On weekends
they read in their rooms until noon
then make brunch for the rest of us,
bran flakes and bananas. They grow up
loved and loving, loud or quiet. They honour music
and water and whatever they find
in an open field. They earn and learn,
find friends and lose them, survive all scares,
all scars. All-stars whatever position
they play, they *always* play,
naming pets after action figures,
action figures after pets and, well,
when I become Poet Laureate,
we do go on about our children.

5.

When I become Poet Laureate, every lover knows
what the other wants, no code-breaking
required, no turning into saps
at first sign of rejection, or assassins when the going
gets tough. Emotions roam peacefully,
advance single-file, serene unless spurred
in acts of love to a high stampede, after which
they settle, and resume grazing.

No book gives sweeter read than *How to Make
Love in Saskatchewan* (Chapter One: *Weather.*
Chapter Two: *Rowboats.* Chapter Three: *~~Mosquitos~~ Mojitos).*
Every scrap of text to or from
the lover carries rapture cut with grit,
not a word clunked or scene fumbled.
The thousand daily tremors
love creates no longer
fool us. We can stop
cleaning house to dull the pain.

When I become Poet Laureate, all poets
who lost their virginity within
municipal boundaries of Regina
erect a heritage plaque noting who
and where and how much liquor it took.

Soon the playgrounds with their wild
and secret beds are riddled with plaques,
and the shores of lake Wascana

and that lonely road south of the airport,
where the poets take off and touch down.
The poet whose name begins with E
plants her plaque on the front steps
of the Legislature until security intervenes
(which it should have done
that June night long ago).

A certain townhouse on 18th avenue bristles
with eight or nine plaques dated winter
of '70-'71, thanks "Heart of Gold" and "Maggie Mae"
and "American Pie" playing
in that third-floor room.

And a formerly barren viewpoint
blooms with plaques for acts of love
committed in parked cars while the sun
rises or sets. Poets will claim for the rest
of their lives no greater thrill
than loving at the lookout
tonight.

6.

When I become Poet Laureate, I keep to myself
the cold theft of a rubber stopper
and tubes from the Chem lab at high school
for the water pipe we made
in our rumpus rooms. I receive from P3
(Prairie Pot Patrol) a pardon
for misdemeanors committed with roach clips and Zig-Zags.

It's known now as pre-smoking,
what we did in our living rooms
on Smith before the Bonnie
and Delaney concert in '72. The way things
are going, medical pot will come
with our bowl of bran flakes
and bananas at sunrise every day
by the time we turn ninety, if we make
that turn, if we want to, if we haven't
let go by then.

7.

When I become Poet Laureate, our bones feel
the lives we've lived. Still
we lift or push or lunge
pretty much as always, swing a bat
or sweep a curling stone,
more than a match for any four
bags of groceries, any spare tire.
We accept the tyranny of aging
on the country of our bodies and see
our future guaranteed pain-free,
no burden on our children or the state.
Lovers years younger still blush
from our tasty flirtations. For laughs
our t-shirts say *miserable old coot*
but we never are. Our minds
stay clear until our last breath
which slips through our lips the very day
the Leafs win the Stanley Cup.

8.

Finally, when I become Poet Laureate,
the Trans-Canada highway flows
through the heart of our hometowns again.
Stores revive, high schools re-open.
Piano recitals (*Fűr Elise*) please the ear,
and girls who drive to Swift Current
the afternoon of grad for hair-dos
make it home ok. Kids who want
to see the world elsewhere go
and come back believing in the power
of stories including their own.

When I become Poet Laureate, we climb
the spiral staircase up the dome
of the Legislature to gaze upon our city
and the countryside. We see no potholes
from here to the border. We see clean water
shining and wild grass, and cities fill in tasteful burbs
that never flood. We see loved ones safely buried.
We see industries of hope and growth
and visitors from other lands sing
in their own voices who they are.
We see ourselves in a land alive.

When I become Poet Laureate,
this is all to be continued.

Crooked at the Far End: Notes

The Title

Crooked at the far end of the journey, idea, hallway, life, hook, line, and stinker.

"Invocation"

An invocation is an ancient device, a prayer for guidance and protection for the journey—in this case, departure from the Wallace Stegner house in Eastend, Saskatchewan. And into the book ahead.

"Eight Souls . . ."

Imagine a cabin at Emma Lake, Saskatchewan. One day I got the idea of hosting guests there, people I admire, all of whom lived between 1927 and 1930. The years don't matter, other than they're the ones I selected, somehow, to limit my choices. It's summer at Emma. The lake is fifty yards away.

"Natural Cause"

Surrounded by artists of all kinds at the Leighton studios of the Banff Centre, I can't help teasing, as much as I love them and derive inspiration from their work and presence.

"Pub Scrawls"

These are written and set south of Edinburgh, the furthest reach of the regional bus service. I wrote more freely away from the Hawthornden house (that some call a castle), where I had a residency, than at it. The many pubs a bus stop or two away, or all the way into the old city, made for dandy work spaces.

"Occasional Cities"

Occasional Cities are built from intersections of sensation and desire. Just as the historical cities of southern Portugal and Spain were shaped by centuries of conquest by Romans, Moors, and Iberians, so my experience of these cities was shaped by reading Josè Saramago, Fernando Pessoa and Federico García Lorca, who all lived there. I saw their cities and wrote mine. Of course, my interest in versions of cities derives from the wonderful *Invisible Cities* of Italo Calvino.

"Songs for Scarborough Bluffs"

The Doris McCarthy house in Scarborough, now an artist retreat administered by Ontario Heritage Trust, saw the birth of these poems. The thirteen acres Doris bought for a song—though I'm sure it took all the money she could muster—overlook Lake Ontario from the blufftops seventy meters up. At every moment, the bluff erodes, and it's not long before one's consciousness turns to matters eternal.

"Writing Wrongs"

For these poems, blame the My Paradise beach club at Puerto Morelos, on the east coast of the Yucatan peninsula, where I spent five or six hours a day for three weeks. And blame Lorca, whose poems and plays—and the fish tacos and sun and bucket of *Modelo Negras*—stirred the afternoons.

"When I Become Poet Laureate"

I wrote this series, for my installation as Poet Laureate in 2016, as a tease—satirizing claims for "the power of poetry" or "why poetry matters." You can find YouTube videos for most of these pieces. Tom Wayman published *Nobel Prize Acceptance Speech* with Thistledown in 1981. My series is an homage to Tom's title poem, in which his "Wayman" character accepts the big prize.

Acknowledgements

Some of these poems appeared, perhaps in different forms with different titles, in the following journals. Thanks to all editors and readers:

"Evening Tram to Rossio" in *Canadian Literature* and "Wrong for the Great-tailed Grackle" and "Mirror" in *Grain*

"Map of Sevilla" and "Moon" in *The Fiddlehead*

"The Easy Flynn", "The Grand-dad Inn", "The Look Back Inn", "The Inn With the Rest of the Names" in *Windsor Review*

"Eight Souls . . ." in *En Route.*

"Wrong About the Road" and "Page of Water" in *The Society.*

Thank you, Wallace Stegner House committee, Saskatchewan Writers/Artists Retreat, the Banff Centre, and Hawthornden International Retreat for Writers for writer-friendly homes away from home.

I'm grateful to the Saskatchewan Arts Board for an Independent Artists Program grant, to Ontario Heritage Trust for my three months as Artist-in-Residence at Fool's Paradise, the Doris McCarthy house in Scarborough, and to Luther College at the University of Regina for a President's Research Fund grant that enabled valuable writing time.

"Eight Souls . . ." won Second Prize for Poetry in the 2011 CBC Literary Awards.

An earlier version of "Song for Scarborough Bluffs" was published in the Olive Reading Series chapbook in 2016, produced by Paul Pearson.

Crooked at the Far End is a title suggested by Phil Hall. Thanks, Phil.

Hayley Peters created the silhouette of the author.

Text in "Virginia Woolf, Writer" is borrowed from Woolf's *Mrs. Dalloway*.

Brenda Schmidt edited this book. I've been wanting this for years. Thank you, Brenda.

And I thank audiences, who in hearing some of these poems, helped shape them.

Gerald Hill lives amid the leafy confines of downtown Regina, Saskatchewan. A two-time winner of the Saskatchewan Book Award for Poetry, Hill was Poet Laureate of Saskatchewan in 2016. His forty-year teaching career took him across western Canada and to Papua New Guinea as a CUSO volunteer, finally to Luther College at the University of Regina, where Hill taught English and Creative Writing until 2018. Meanwhile, he maintained an active literary life as a writer published in over 35 journals, literary festival presenter, event organizer, editor, leader, conference speaker, grant recipient, and mentor. Among the highlights: Instructor, Writing With Style, The Banff Centre, 2011; Writer-in-Residence, Convento São Francisco de Mértola, Portugal, February, 2010; Fellow, Hawthornden Retreat for Writers, Lasswade, Scotland, April, 2010; Resident, Leighton Studios, The Banff Centre, 2007, 2009, 2012, 2013; Resident, Wallace Stegner House, Eastend, Sask., 2007, 2009; Poetry Editor, *Grain*, 2003-2008. *Crooked at the Far End* is his 7th poetry collection.